ESSAYS
LETTERS
REPORTS

Sandra Panman
SUNY, College at New Paltz

Richard Panman, Ph.D.
SUNY, College at New Paltz

Active Learning Corporation
New Paltz, New York
(914) 255-0844

Essays/Letters/Reports

Address all inquiries to:
Active Learning Corporation
P.O. Box 254
New Paltz, New York 12561
(914) 255-0844

Text Design, Editing and Montage: Linda Gluck
Art Director, Illustrations: Elena Erber
Illustrators: Kirk Van Deusen, Marco Paz

Printed in the United States of America/vg92
ISBN: 0-912813-15-6

Acknowledgements:

Thomas Stewart Brush: "Birthday Party" by Katharine Brush, copyright © 1946, by Katharine Brush. Originally published in *The New Yorker*, March 16, 1946.

E.B. White: Excerpt from "Once More to the Lake" from *Essays of E.B. White*. Copyright 1941 by E.B. White. Reprinted by permission of Harper & Row, Publishers, Inc.

Contents

How To Use This Book

Essays/Letters/Reports consists of writing guides grouped into three major categories. Each guide clearly specifies what is to be learned and how to master the task. These guides teach the kind of writing often required on the job, in school, and in your personal life. The goal of this book is to teach you the skills necessary to write essays, letters, and reports with ease and confidence.

Letters come in many forms. A letter may be used as an introduction when applying for a job or requesting an interview. This cover letter is sent along with a resume when you are seeking employment. The resume, a summary of your accomplishments, and the cover letter are the first two lessons in this book. The next two guides teach how to write other business letters. People often write letters to order by mail, as well as to complain when they are dissatisfied with what they receive. The business letter format can be used whenever you have to communicate in a formal way.

The section on essays begins with an introduction that explains the structure of the essay, followed by brief definitions that distinguish each strategy from the others. The narrative essay is a story that makes a point. The descriptive essay creates vivid impressions for the reader. The expository essay explains or informs. The persuasive essay tries to convince the reader to see things a certain way.

The report section focuses on gathering, organizing and presenting information. The Short Report guide will teach you to write in an organized and informative manner. Report writing often requires you to explain facts and ideas so that they are easily understood. This guide can be used to write reports about science, history, people, places and current events.

Students are often asked to write a report based on a novel. The Book Report guide presented here offers a step-by-step plan for gathering information and writing this report. In writing the book report, you will make use of two important strategies: narration and description. Narration involves telling a story, while description is used to create vivid impressions for the reader.

The skills you have acquired in writing the short report are also applicable to the research paper. While the form of both is the same, the research paper has more development paragraphs. Knowing how to write a research paper is essential in school and useful in many occupations.

Each guide in the book begins with a model of the type of writing you will learn to master. Read the model and complete the Practice exercises that follow. These prewriting activities teach the skills necessary to write paragraphs (answer key included). Follow the plan or outline provided in each lesson to write your first draft. Use the Checklist as a way of evaluating and revising your work before you submit it to the teacher for review.

If you are using this book on your own, outside of a classroom setting, no teacher will be available to evaluate your work. Ask a person whose opinion you respect—friend, colleague, or relative—to read your papers and give you feedback. Ask them to tell you what they learned from your paper, what they liked and disliked about it, and what was clear or unclear about the paper. Make revisions based on their comments and the Checklist in each lesson.

To The Teacher

"How to Use This Book" provides an overview of the text for both student and teacher. In addition, several points relevant mainly to the instructor are grouped together here. These concern coordinating outside readings with the text, guidelines for instructor feedback, and suggestions for brainstorming and peer critiquing.

Each guide in this book asks the student to write at least one composition. The Narrative Essay, The Descriptive Essay, The Expository Essay, The Persuasive Essay, and The Short Report all require a second composition based on available fiction and nonfiction reading materials.The teacher can assign, or direct students to, reading materials at their own level. We suggest that students keep all work in a looseleaf binder or writing folder. Upon completion of this text, students will have compiled a visible record of their work and progress in your class.

Feedback from the teacher can have a very powerful and positive effect in motivating the student to learn. Make sure students understand your system for evaluating and grading papers. To gain students' trust and confidence, try to give them the good news first, followed by your constructive criticism. The good news is praise for at least one aspect of the student's paper: ideas, choice of subject, enthusiasm, neat handwriting, etc.

When there are many errors in a paper, focus on three or four of the most frequent ones. As these are eliminated, you can point out others. Try not to overwhelm your students with criticism before they develop confidence in their ability to write. Written comments should be specific enough for the student to make changes and corrections in their work. You may also want to speak with the student in a brief, one-to-one informal conference in class. Conferences allow for discussion and direct exchange of ideas.

Two valuable and enjoyable classroom activities that you can use with the text are brainstorming and peer critiquing. While composition exercises provide suggested topics, you may wish to have students "brainstorm" as a group to generate other topics. From time to time, completed compositions can be critiqued by the peer group. Prepare students for this by sharing the feedback guidelines above and encouraging constructive criticism. Peer critiquing gives students an opportunity to sharpen their listening and speaking skills, as well as improve writing ability.

ESSAYS
LETTERS
REPORTS

Preparing a Resume

This guide will help you to write a resume. A clearly written resume can be a real advantage when you are looking for a job. The primary purpose of a resume is to get you an interview. A resume summarizes information about your life experiences and conveys a picture of you as a person. By preparing a resume, you show a prospective employer that you want to make a good first impression.

There are many ways to use your resume, as the following list illustrates:

- answering ads
- sending it to organizations where you seek employment
- distributing it to friends, family, or other acquaintances for networking
- giving it to a person writing a letter of reference for you
- attaching it to a job application

Practice

Read the sample resume, then complete the exercise that follows. This part of the guide will help to organize the data necessary to write your own resume.

RESUME

Renee Osborne
25 West 98th Street, New York, N.Y. 10071   (212) 315-8022

Career Goal

I am interested in challenging work with children as a teacher and counselor.

Work Experience

Counselor — YMCA Day Camp, New York, N.Y.
6/89–8/89   Supervised and coordinated activities of handicapped girls, ages 10-12.

Volunteer — West End Day Care Center, New York, N.Y.
6/88–8/88   Supervised games and activities of youngsters, ages 2-4.

Education

9/89 —   City College of New York, New York, N.Y.

9/86–6/89   Louis D. Brandeis High School, New York, N.Y. Regents Diploma

Special Skills

Typing, American sign language, piano

Interests and Hobbies

Swimming, music, running, photography

Awards and Achievements

Honor Society, Service Award, Lifesaving Certificate

References

Ms. Valerie Fernandez
Director, YMCA Day Camp
2010 Richmond Street
New York, N.Y. 10002

Dr. James Palmer
Department of Psychology
City College of New York
New York, N.Y. 10034

Once you provide all of the information requested below, you will be ready to write your own resume.

Identification Heading

This information is presented at the top of the page.

1. Your name _____

2. Street address _____

3. City, state, and zip code _____

4. Telephone number (   ) ___ _____

Career Goal

What do you want to be? Express your long-range career goals in terms of the education you wish to attain and/or the work you want to do.

5. _____

In the sample resume, WORK EXPERIENCE is presented first, followed by EDUCATION. The order of these categories is interchangeable; the one you wish to emphasize comes first. In either case, your most **recent** accomplishment is listed **first.** Other experiences follow in reverse order, from present to past.

Work Experience

How many jobs will you be listing on your resume? If you've had many jobs, list those you've held the longest and those that are most relevant to the work you are now seeking. You may have received pay for some, and volunteered your services at others. For each position, provide the data as requested in items 6-10 below. Your most recent job is listed first.

6. Job title: _____

7. Name of employer (agency or company):

   _____

8. Location of employment (city and state only):

   _____

9. Job responsibilities (complete sentences not necessary):

   _____

10. Dates of employment (give month and year you began work, and month and year the job ended):

    _____ to _____

Education

List the secondary and postsecondary schools you have attended: high school, college, career institute, etc. Begin with your most recent experience and work backwards.

11. Name of school _____

12. Location (city and state) _____

13. Degree granted _____

14. Dates attended (month and year) _____ to _____

The next three categories pertain to your skills, interests, hobbies, and special achievements. You may have data to include for all three categories, just two categories, or only one. If you have no data for a category, eliminate that category from your resume.

Special Skills

A skill is an ability in which you have demonstrated competence. You can do it well. For example, a measure of typing skill is expressed by the number of words you can type, per minute, without error.

There are other skills in which competence is measured by a successful outcome. The ability to maintain or repair the engine so that your car runs well is a valuable skill to have.

15. List your skills:

_____

Interests and Hobbies

An interest is something that holds our attention over a period of time. We become actively involved with an interest or hobby because the activity is rewarding. Some examples are: swimming, basketball, dancing, music, photography, and drawing.

When you develop competence in an interest, you have acquired a new skill. When you start swimming competitively on a team, your hobby is now a skill. When your musical ability leads you to performing with a band on weekends, your interest has become a skill.

16. List your interests and hobbies:

_____

Awards and Achievements

17. List awards, honors, certificates, and other formal recognition of your accomplishments:

_____

References

A prospective employer may want to contact people who know you and can provide a reference. Employers usually ask for information which includes:

- verification of your education and work experience.

- previous job evaluations.

- assessment of your character.

It is to your advantage to have positive references. Before you list someone, ask that person directly if they would agree to provide a reference for you. Do ask: teachers, guidance counselors, previous employers, neighbors, your physician, or minister. References from relatives are not recommended. List at least **two** references.

18. Name of reference _____

    Agency or company (if applicable):

    _____

    Address of reference (business or residence):

    _____

    City, state and zip code:

    _____

Once you have completed the Practice exercise, go on to the Composition part of this guide.

Composition

In this part of the guide you will be writing your own resume. Refer to the model as you present your information. Type the final copy of your resume on unlined bond paper.

Use the Checklist to help you review and revise your writing. Do this for all drafts and your final copy.

Checklist   Yes   No

1. I used information I provided in the Practice exercise to write my resume.   _____   _____

2. I followed the format of the sample resume.   _____   _____

3. The Identification Heading is at the top of the page.   _____   _____

4. My work and educational experiences are listed in reverse chronological order, from present to past.   _____   _____

5. I included special skills, interests, and awards where relevant.   _____   _____

6. I proofread and edited my resume.   _____   _____

7. I typed the final copy of my resume on unlined bond paper.   _____   _____

Submit the completed writing assignment and Practice exercise to your instructor for evaluation.

Business Letter: Employment

This guide will help you to write a business letter. The focus of your writing will be a letter of application for a job. In it, you can introduce yourself and request an interview. This letter accompanies your resume when writing to a prospective employer.

Cover letters use the business letter format, as shown in the model. The six parts of the letter are labeled as follows:

HEADING

INSIDE ADDRESS

GREETING

BODY

CLOSING

SIGNATURE

Practice

Read each part of the following exercise and answer all **24** questions. Begin with the model cover letter on the next page.

Heading —
25 West 98th Street
New York, N.Y. 10071
September 15, 1990

Ms. Martha Robbins
The New Day Residence
P.O. Box 2047
Brooklyn, New York 12249
Inside Address

Dear Ms. Robbins: **Greeting**

I am writing to apply for the position of part-time Resident Assistant which was listed with the Career Placement Office at City College.

I worked with handicapped children in a previous job at the YMCA Day Camp. I found this experience very rewarding. I was also a volunteer at a day care center. I like working with youngsters and plan to make a career of teaching and counseling children.

B
o
d
y

I have enclosed a resume which summarizes my experiences and qualifications. I would like to have the opportunity to discuss this position in a personal interview, and would be pleased to meet you at your convenience. I can be reached evenings at (212) 315-8022.

Closing — Sincerely,

Signature — *Renee Osborne*
Renee Osborne

Enc.

For the following exercise, write the **letter** of the phrase that best completes each sentence.

1. _____ The address in the **heading** belongs to the person:

   a. writing the letter.

   b. reading the letter.

2. _____ The **inside address** belongs to the person:

   a. writing the letter.

   b. receiving the letter.

3. _____ The **greeting** is directed at the person:

   a. writing the letter.

   b. receiving the letter.

4. _____ The **body** of the letter gives information about the person:

   a. writing the letter.

   b. receiving the letter.

5. _____ The **closing** of the business letter is sincere, yet formal. Which of the following would *not* be an appropriate closing?

   a. Yours truly,

   b. Respectfully,

   c. Sincerely,

   d. Your friend,

6. _____ The writer's **signature** appears:

    a. in the heading.

    b. after the closing.

The following list includes the kind of information presented in the model letter. This information can be grouped and ordered into three paragraphs: introduction, middle, and conclusion. For each phrase, write the letter *A* if the information appears in the first paragraph, *B* if it appears in the second paragraph, or *C* if it appears in the third paragraph.

7. _____ reference to enclosed resume

8. _____ the position applied for

9. _____ relevant career goals

10. _____ why you are writing

11. _____ request for an interview

12. _____ reasons for wanting this job

13. _____ how you heard of the opening

14. _____ how you can be reached

15. _____ qualifications to do this work

Now that you have grouped this information by paragraph, write each phrase in the appropriate order according to the outline below.

A. Introductory Paragraph

16. _____

17. _____

18. _____

B. Middle Paragraph

19. _____

20. _____

21. _____

C. Concluding Paragraph

22. _____

23. _____

24. _____

Score the Practice exercise using the Answer Key, and go on to the Composition part of this guide.

Composition

This part of the guide will help you to apply what you have learned about writing a business letter. Write a letter in which you introduce yourself and request a job interview. On the next page is a list of six job openings. You may write to any one of these, or respond to an actual job advertisement. Use the outline that follows the job listings. Type or write the final copy of your letter.

Job Openings

Part-time road worker
Ace Asphalt Paving Company
6300 South Dixie Highway
Jacksonville, Florida 32250

Punch key operator—will train
Evenings and weekends
Computer Data Systems
800 Delaware Avenue
Cleveland, Ohio 44108

Salesclerk—flexible hours, good benefits
Gap Stores, Inc.
8323 W. Spruce Street
Dallas, Texas 75281

Food concession—weekends and summer season
Taco Don's Inc.
One Towers Drive
Los Angeles, California 90011

Part-time receptionist
Maxim's Beauty Salon
2049 Century Park
Atlanta, Georgia 30309

Guided Tours, Inc.
1011 West Washington Street
Chicago, Illinois 60607

Follow the business letter format. Use *Dear Sir or Madam:* as your greeting if the name of the person doing the hiring is not known. Follow the outline below and refer to the model in the Practice exercise as you write your letter.

Outline

I. Introductory Paragraph

    A. Tell why you are writing.

    B. State the position applied for.

    C. Indicate how you heard of the opening.

II. Middle Paragraph

    A. Give your qualifications for this work.

    B. State your reasons for wanting this job.

    C. Refer to your relevant career goals.

III. Concluding Paragraph

    A. Refer to the enclosed resume.

    B. Request a personal interview.

    C. Tell how you can be reached.

Below the signature of your letter, at the left margin, you may want to include additional information such as *Enc.* (something is enclosed with the letter), or *cc: Jack Butler* (a carbon copy is being sent to the person named).

The envelope for the letter should show your name and address in the upper left corner and the addressee's name, title, and address in the center.

Use the Checklist to help you review and revise your writing. Do this for all drafts and your final copy.

Checklist   Yes   No

1. I wrote a letter of application introducing myself and requesting a job interview.   _____ _____

2. I used the business letter format as presented in the model.   _____ _____

3. The body of my letter contains three paragraphs. I explain why I am writing, give my qualifications, my reasons for wanting the job, and request an interview.   _____ _____

4. I used transitions to connect ideas and create unity in my writing.   _____ _____

5. I proofread and edited my business letter.   _____ _____

6. I typed or wrote a corrected copy of my work.   _____ _____

Submit the completed writing assignment and Practice exercise to your instructor for evaluation.

Business Letter: Ordering

This guide will help you to understand how to order merchandise by letter. The business letter format is always the same, regardless of your purpose; however, the kind of information that goes into the body of the letter will change.

Practice

Read each part of the following exercise and answer all **38** questions. Begin with the model letter on the next page in which Ben Franklin orders a kite.

Heading — 823 Stonybrook Road
Philadelphia, Pennsylvania 19132
July 7, 1990

Fly by Night Novelties
2468 Adventure Avenue
San Francisco, California 90083 — **Inside Address**

Dear Sir or Madam: — **Greeting**

I would like to order one blue silk kite, model number K3.
Please print the following words on the kite in day-glo
orange, at no extra charge:

B
o
d
YOU'RE THE BEST!
y

I have enclosed a check for $10 to cover the cost of the kite,
plus postage and handling. Please send this order via
"Speedy Service" as advertised.

Closing — Sincerely,

Signature — *Ben Franklin*

Ben Franklin

Enc.

Select words from the list to fill in the blanks below. Refer to the model letter to help you complete this exercise. Some words will be used more than once.

name	day	two	: (colon)
year	zip code	state	street address
body	cities	closing	capital letters
sent	explains	date	Dear Sir or Madam
sign	greeting	product	inside address
cost	comma	signature	lower case letter

The Heading Questions 1-8 refer to the heading of the letter.

1. The first line of the heading is the _____ of the person who is writing the letter.

2. The second line of the heading contains the city, _____, and zip code.

3. Names of streets, cities, and states always begin with _____.

4. There is always a _____ after the name of the city.

5. The _____ appears after the name of the state.

6. The _____ always appears on the third line of the heading.

7. The date includes the month, the day, and the _____.

8. A comma is placed between the _____ and the year.

The Inside Address Questions 9-12 refer to the inside address of the letter.

9. Skip at least two lines after the heading and begin the _____.

10. The _____ of the company is the first line of the inside address. (If you are writing to a specific individual, that name will appear on the first line. The company name will appear on the second line.)

11. Names of streets, _____, and states begin with capital letters.

12. The zip code appears after the name of the _____.

The Greeting Questions 13-15 refer to the greeting of the letter.

13. Skip three lines after the inside address and write the _____.

14. Unless you have an individual's name, use the words _____ as your greeting.

15. The greeting always ends with a _____.

The Body Questions 16-21 refer to the body of the letter.

16. Skip three lines after the greeting and begin the _____ of the letter.

17. The body is the part of the letter which _____ why you are writing.

18. The body of this letter contains _____ paragraphs.

19. The first paragraph contains specific information relating to the _____ that is being ordered.

20. The second paragraph contains information about the _____ of the product and where it is to be

21. _____.

The Closing   Questions 22-24 refer to the closing of the letter.

22. Skip three lines after the body of the letter and write the
    _____.

23. Closings such as *Sincerely, Sincerely yours,* and *Yours truly,* are always followed by a _____.

24. When a closing has two words, such as *Sincerely yours,* or *Yours truly,* the second word begins with a _____.

The Signature   Questions 25-26 refer to the signature of the letter.

25. Skip five lines after the closing and type or print your full name. This insures that the reader will know the spelling of your name. _____ your name in the space between the closing and your typed or printed name.

26. Both your signed name and your typed or printed name are referred to as the _____.

The following list includes the kind of information provided in the model letter. This information can be grouped and ordered into two paragraphs. For each phrase, write the letter *A* if the information appears in the first paragraph, or *B* if it appears in the second paragraph.

27. _____ how you plan to pay for merchandise (check, credit card, money order, C.O.D.)

28. _____ special instructions, if any (color, size, inscription)

29. _____ brief description of product, including model or reference number (if given)

30. _____ indicate the product you are ordering

31. _____ reference to postage and handling

32. _____ how you would like product shipped (if there is a choice)

Now that you have grouped the information by paragraphs, write each phrase in the appropriate order according to the outline below.

A. Opening Paragraph

33. _____

34. _____

35. _____

B. Closing Paragraph

36. _____

37. _____

38. _____

Score the Practice exercise using the Answer Key, and go on to the Composition part of this guide.

Composition

This part of the guide will help you to apply what you have learned about ordering merchandise by letter. Respond to one of the following advertisements. Ads like these appear regularly in newspapers and magazines. Use the outline presented to help you write your letter. Type or write the final copy of your letter.

Advertisements

AMAZING JEWELRY OFFER! 14 karat gold chains—16″, 18″, 20″. Chains incredibly priced at $49.95, $59.95, and $69.95. Please specify size. Add $2.50 for postage, handling, and insurance. Send check or money order to: Marvelous Metals, Inc., 3034 Woodward Avenue, Detroit, Michigan 48271.

SUPER SHIRT SPECIAL! 100% cotton T-shirts in your choice of color. $6 each! Up to six words printed free. Write desired inscription in block letters. Specify shirt **color:** red, blue, yellow, black, or white and **size:** small, medium, large, Xlarge. Add $1.95 for shipping and handling. Allow six weeks for delivery. For *rush* service, include additional $1.00. Send check, money order, or credit card number to: Shirt Special, P.O. Box 1950, Houston, Texas 77053.

PARTY FAVORS! Order unique party favors by mail at discount prices! Guaranteed to keep your friends laughing. Assorted balloon figures—politicians, movie stars, and cartoon characters—$7.95 per hundred; offbeat noisemakers, ten for $7.50; set of magic tricks, $5.95. Add 10% for postage and handling. Send check or money order to: Fantasy Fun, Inc., P.O. Box 31, Denver, Colorado 80215

Outline

I. Opening Paragraph

   A. State the product you are ordering.

   B. Give a brief description of product, including model or reference number (if given).

C. Provide special instructions, such as color, size, or inscription.

II. Closing Paragraph

    A. Tell how you plan to pay for merchandise (check, credit card, money order, C.O.D.)

    B. Make reference to payment for postage and handling.

    C. State how you would like product shipped, if there is a choice.

Use the Checklist to help you review and revise your writing. Do this for all drafts and your final copy.

Checklist   Yes   No

1. I wrote a letter in which I ordered merchandise.   ____   ____

2. I used the business letter format.   ____   ____

3. The body of my letter contains two paragraphs. I describe the product, include special instructions, and make payment and shipping arrangements.   ____   ____

4. I used transitions to connect ideas and create unity in my writing.   ____   ____

5. I proofread and edited my business letter.   ____   ____

6. I typed or wrote the final copy of my work.   ____   ____

Submit the completed writing assignment and Practice exercise to your instructor for evaluation.

Business Letter: Complaint

This guide will help you to understand how to write a letter of complaint. When you are dissatisfied with a product or a service, you may want to register a complaint with the seller in a formal way. You are more likely to get a response and quick resolution to the problem if you put it in writing.

Practice

Read each part of the following exercise and answer all **12** questions.

On July 4th, Benjamin Franklin ordered a blue silk kite, model number K3. The words, "YOU'RE THE BEST!" were to be inscribed in day-glo orange. The cost of the kite, plus postage and handling, was ten dollars.

On July 20th, he received the kite with the words, "YOU'RE THE BEAST!" written in bright orange on the material. The letter of complaint he wrote about this problem appears on the next page.

823 Stonybrook Road
Philadelphia, Pennsylvania 19132
July 22, 1990

Fly by Night Novelties
2468 Adventure Avenue
San Francisco, California 90083

Dear Sir or Madam:

On July 4, 1990, I ordered a blue silk kite, model number K3. I asked that the words "YOU'RE THE BEST!" be inscribed in day-glo orange. I sent you a check for ten dollars to cover the cost of the kite, plus postage and handling.

On July 20th, I received the kite as ordered, with the words "YOU'RE THE BEAST!" written in bright orange. The kite is fine, but I don't think the inscription is suitable as a gift the way it is. I am returning the kite and ask that you send me a new one, with the words "YOU'RE THE BEST!" written on it. Please rush this so I can have it by August 8th, in time for my wife's birthday.

Sincerely,

Ben Franklin

Ben Franklin

The following list includes the kind of information presented in the model letter of complaint. This information can be grouped and ordered into two paragraphs. For each phrase, write the letter *A* if the information appears in the first paragraph, or the letter *B* if it appears in the second paragraph.

1. _____ cost of product, including shipping

2. _____ date you received product

3. _____ what you want the seller to do

4. _____ description of product received, including defects

5. _____ date you ordered product

6. _____ detailed description of product ordered, including model number

Now that you have grouped the information by paragraph, write each phrase in the appropriate order according to the outline below.

Outline

A. Opening Paragraph

    7. _____

    8. _____

    9. _____

B. Closing Paragraph

    10. _____

    11. _____

    12. _____

Score the Practice exercise using Answer Key, and go on to the Composition part of this guide.

Composition

This part of the guide will help you to apply what you have learned about writing a letter of complaint. In the last guide, you responded to one of several advertisements by ordering a product. Below is a list of problems which occurred with each of the products ordered. Write a letter of complaint about the product that you ordered using the information and the outline provided. Type or write the final copy of your letter.

Problems

- The 14 karat gold chain you ordered turned out to be gold filled (dipped in gold, but not solid).

- The 100% cotton T-shirt you ordered for yourself shrank to half its size in the first washing.

- You ordered all three party favors advertised. You received the magic tricks and the noisemakers, but not the balloons.

Outline

I. Opening Paragraph

   A. Identify the product and give the date it was ordered.

   B. Provide a detailed description of product ordered, including model number.

   C. Indicate the cost of the product; include shipping charges.

II. Closing Paragraph

    A. Give the date you received product.

    B. Describe the product received, including defects.

    C. State what you want the seller to do about this problem.

Use the Checklist to help you review and revise your writing. Do this for all drafts and your final copy.

Checklist   Yes   No

1. I wrote a letter of complaint about my order to the seller.   _____   _____

2. I used the business letter format.   _____   _____

3. The body of my letter contains two paragraphs. The first paragraph tells what I ordered. The second paragraph tells what I received and what I want the seller to do.   _____   _____

4. I used transitions to connect ideas and create unity in my writing.   _____   _____

5. I proofread and edited my business letter.   _____   _____

6. I typed or wrote the final copy of my work.   _____   _____

Submit the completed writing assignment and Practice exercise to your instructor for evaluation.

The Essay

The next four guides in this book will help you to write essays using different strategies: narration, description, exposition, and persuasion. The basic structure of each essay consists of an introductory paragraph, one or more development paragraphs, and a concluding paragraph.

The first paragraph introduces the topic of the essay and indicates a plan for its development. The middle paragraph or paragraphs develop the topic with supporting details: facts, descriptions, examples, and opinions. The concluding paragraph restates the topic and summarizes the main points of the essay.

You can use the format of the essay to:

- tell a story (narrate)
- create vivid images for the reader by appealing to the five senses (describe)
- present facts and ideas so they are easily understood (explain)
- convince the reader to see things your way (persuade)

The guides to writing essays are followed by several guides to writing reports. Both essays and reports involve organizing information and presenting it in a logical way, so that it makes sense to your reader. Essays allow for the personal expression of opinions and beliefs while reports focus on the presentation of facts. Mastering the concepts presented in these lessons will make you a better reader, a better writer, and ultimately a better student.

The Narrative Essay

A narrative tells a story that makes a point. All narratives have the common elements of setting, plot, and point of view. The **setting** of a narrative is the time and place of the story. The **plot** is the sequence of events in the story through which the author tells what is happening, to whom, and why. **Point of view** identifies the position of the storyteller. A first-person narrator is a character in the story, while a third-person narrator tells what is happening from a position outside the story.

The model narrative titled "Birthday Party" is a short, short story written by Katharine Brush. The author tells about an experience she had in a restaurant. These every day events can often go unnoticed, but a keen observer of human behavior can make the ordinary interesting. Read the model and answer all **18** questions in the exercise that follows.

They were a couple in their late thirties, and they looked unmistakably married. They sat on the banquette opposite us in a little narrow restaurant, having dinner. The man had a round, self-satisfied face, with glasses on it; the woman was fadingly pretty, in a big hat. There was nothing conspicuous about them, nothing particularly noticeable, until the end of their meal, when it suddenly became obvious that this was an Occasion—in fact, the husband's birthday, and the wife had planned a little surprise for him.

It arrived, in the form of a small but glossy birthday cake, with one pink candle burning in the center. The headwaiter brought it in and placed it before the husband, and meanwhile the violin-and-piano orchestra played "Happy Birthday to You" and the wife beamed with shy pride over her little surprise, and such few people as there were in the restaurant tried to help out with a pattering of applause. It became clear at once that help was needed, because the husband was not pleased. Instead he was hotly embarrassed, and indignant at his wife for embarrassing him.

You looked at him and you saw this and you thought, "Oh, now, don't *be* like that!" But he was like that, and as soon as the little cake had been deposited on the table, and the orchestra had finished the birthday piece, and the general attention had shifted from the man and woman, I saw him say something to her under his breath—some punishing thing, quick and curt and unkind. I couldn't bear to look at the woman then, so I stared at my plate and waited for quite a long time. Not long enough, though. She was still crying when I finally glanced over there again. Crying quietly and heartbrokenly and hopelessly, all to herself, under the gay big brim of her best hat.

The Introductory Paragraph

The first sentence should get the attention of the reader in some way. This story begins by introducing the setting and the characters, making us want to know more about them.

1. Where does the story take place?

2. Who is the story about?

3. The couple is sitting on a banquette. What is a *banquette*?

4. Where is the narrator in this story?

5. Is this a first or third person narrative, and why?

6. What is the couple doing?

7. Why is this night special for the couple?

The Development Paragraph

The development paragraph provides details about the characters and what is happening to them. In this paragraph the author builds the plot and leads the reader toward the point of the story.

8. What was delivered to the couple's table at the end of the meal?

9. What did the violin-and-piano orchestra do?

10. How did the wife feel about her surprise?

11. What did the other customers in the restaurant do?

12. How did the husband feel about the surprise?

13. Define the word *indignant* as used in this narrative?

Concluding Paragraph

At the end of this paragraph the reader understands the point of the story. The last paragraph may summarize what the story is about, express a reaction to what has happened, offer an opinion, or reach a conclusion about what has happened. The author of the model narrative leaves the reader with an image of the lady crying, from which we can draw certain conclusions.

14. Write the sentence that expresses the narrator's reaction to the husband's behavior.
15. What does the husband say to his wife under his breath?
16. What is the reaction of the narrator?
17. What is the reaction of the wife?
18. What is your reaction to the husband?

Score the Practice exercise using the Answer Key, and go on to the Composition part of this guide.

Composition

This part of the guide will help you apply what you have learned about writing a narrative essay. Write your essay about **one** of the topics listed below. Follow the outline to write your composition.

Topics

   my encounter with an alien being
   the time I won a prize
   my favorite Halloween story
   I watched with amazement as . . .
   an experience I'll never forget

Outline

I. The Introductory Paragraph

    A. Begin your essay with a sentence that gets the reader's attention.

    B. Introduce the setting, the time and place of your story.

    C. Introduce the characters, their situation, and the position of the narrator in the story.

II. The Development Paragraph

    A. Provide details about the characters and what is happening to them.

    B. Include such details as facts, descriptions, examples, and opinions.

    C. The information you give should build the plot and lead toward the point you are making in this story.

III. The Concluding Paragraph

    A. Let the reader know the point of your essay, either directly or indirectly.

    B. As the narrator, let the reader know your feelings about what is happening or has happened.

    C. Let the reader know the outcome of the story by summarizing, offering an opinion, or drawing a conclusion that reinforces the point of the essay.

Use the Checklist to help you review and revise your writing. Do this for all drafts and your final copy.

Checklist

	Yes	No
1. In my introductory paragraph, I appeal to the reader's interest, introduce the setting, the characters, their situation, and the position of the narrator.	——	——
2. In my development paragraph, I provide details about the characters which help build the plot and lead to the point of the story.	——	——
3. In my concluding paragraph, I let the reader know the outcome of the story by summarizing, offering an opinion, or drawing a conclusion that reinforces the point of the essay.	——	——
4. I used transitions to connect ideas and create unity in my writing.	——	——
5. I wrote complete sentences that begin with capital letters and used proper end punctuation.	——	——
6. I proofread and edited my composition.	——	——
7. I wrote a corrected copy of my work.	——	——

Submit the completed writing assignment and Practice exercise to your instructor for evaluation.

Composition

This section of the guide provides additional practice in writing a narrative essay. Choose a fiction or nonfiction selection to read from available book titles. Write a narrative essay in which you tell a story that makes a point. Follow the outline provided in this lesson to write your composition. Use the checklist to help you review and revise your writing.

The Descriptive Essay

Description is used to create impressions that are vivid, real, and lifelike for the reader. The writer appeals to the five senses by telling us how something looks, tastes, smells, sounds, and feels to the touch. These are five ways of describing a person, place, thing, or idea.

You can describe something objectively, just as it appears, without interpreting it for the reader. Or, you can describe something subjectively, expressing your feelings so that the reader is affected emotionally by your description.

Practice

The model is an excerpt from "Once More to the Lake," a short story by E.B. White. The author's use of description helps us to see what he sees and feel what he feels. Read the model and answer all **36** questions in the exercise that follows. In the model, the narrator describes the things he most enjoyed during his week at camp.

We had a good week at the camp. The bass were biting well and the sun shone endlessly, day after day. We would be tired at night and lie down in the accumulated heat of the little bedrooms after the long hot day and the breeze would stir almost imperceptibly outside and the smell of the swamp drift in through the rusty screens. Sleep would come easily and in the morning the red squirrel would be on the roof, tapping out his gay routine. I kept remembering everything, lying in bed in the mornings—the small steamboat and how quietly she ran on the moonlight sails, when the older boys played their mandolins and the girls sang and we ate doughnuts dipped in sugar, and how sweet the music was on the water in the shining night, and what it had felt like to think about girls then.

After breakfast we would go up to the store and the things were in the same place—the minnows in a bottle, the plugs and spinners disarranged and pawed over by the youngsters from the boys' camp, the fig newtons and the Beeman's gum. Outside, the road was tarred and cars stood in front of the store. Inside, all was just as it had always been, except there was more Coca Cola and not so much Moxie and root beer and birch beer and sarsaparilla. We would walk out with a bottle of pop apiece and sometimes the pop would backfire up our noses and hurt.

One afternoon while we were there at that lake a thunderstorm came up. It was like the revival of an old melodrama that I had seen long ago with childish awe. This was the big scene, still the big scene. The whole thing was so familiar, the first feeling of oppression and heat and a general air around camp of not wanting to go very far away. In midafternoon a curious darkening of the sky, and a lull in everything that had made life tick. Then the kettle drum, then the snare, then the bass drum and cymbals, then crackling light against the dark, and the gods grinning and licking their chops in the hills. Afterward the calm, the rain steadily rustling in the calm lake, the return of light and hope and spirits, and the campers running out in joy and relief to go swimming in the rain.

The Introductory Paragraph

The first sentence of the paragraph, "We had a good week at camp," gets the attention of the reader by telling us what the essay is about. The narrator then uses vivid details to introduce the setting and create a mood. Words and phrases from this paragraph are listed below. Decide which sense is being appealed to in each: sight, sound, smell, taste, or touch.

1. the bass were biting
2. the sun shone endlessly
3. the accumulated heat of the little bedrooms
4. the long hot day and the breeze
5. the smell of the swamp drifts in
6. rusty screens
7. red squirrel
8. tapping out his gay routine
9. how quietly she (steamboat) ran
10. moonlight sails
11. boys played their mandolins
12. girls sang
13. we ate donuts dipped in sugar
14. how sweet the music was
15. water in the shining night

The Development Paragraph

The first paragraph described a variety of things that happened during the week at camp, providing a general overview. In this second paragraph, the writer focuses on one event as he describes a visit to the local store. As in the exercise for the first paragraph, decide which sense is being appealed to in each of the words and phrases below.

16. breakfast

17. minnows in a bottle

18. plugs and spinners disarranged

19. pawed over by the youngsters

20. fig newtons and Beeman's gum

21. road was tarred

22. cars stood in front of the store

23. Coca Cola, Moxie, root beer, birch beer, sarsaparilla

24. the pop would backfire up our noses and hurt

The Concluding Paragraph

In the concluding paragraph, the author describes a dramatic event which builds to a conclusion. In doing so, he makes us feel the fears and joys of the campers. Decide which sense is being appealed to in each of the words and phrases below.

25. thunderstorm

26. an old melodrama that I had seen

27. the first feeling of oppression and heat

28. a curious darkening of the sky

29. a lull in everything that had made life tick

30. the kettle drum, the snare, the bass drum, and cymbals

31. crackling light against the dark

32. the gods grinning

33. and licking their chops

34. rain steadily rustling in the calm lake

35. return of light

36. swimming in the rain

Score the Practice exercise using the Answer Key, and go on to the Composition part of this guide.

Composition

This part of the guide will help you apply what you have learned about writing a descriptive essay. Write your essay about **one** of the topics listed below. Follow the outline to write your composition.

Topics

walking in the rain
my version of paradise
fireworks on July 4th
Thanksgiving dinner
an everyday occurrence in nature

Outline

I. The Introductory Paragraph
   A. Begin your essay with a sentence that introduces your topic and gets the readers attention.
   B. Use vivid details to introduce the setting and create a mood for your essay.
   C. Appeal to the five senses often: sight, sound, smell, taste, and touch. Using description, provide a general overview of your topic.

II. The Development Paragraph
   A. Choose one aspect of your topic to focus on: a person, place, or thing.
   B. Use one, two, or three of the five senses to describe your subject in this paragraph.
   C. Include as many details as possible so that you paint a picture with your words.

III. The Concluding Paragraph
   A. Let the reader know how you feel about the person, place, or thing you are describing.
   B. Using description, discuss those details about the subject that make you feel this way.
   C. Summarize or draw a conclusion that reinforces the point of this essay.

Use the Checklist to help you review and revise your writing. Do this for all drafts and your final copy.

Checklist

	Yes	No
1. In my introductory paragraph, I get the reader's attention, use vivid details, and appeal to the five senses often.	____	____
2. In my development paragraph, I focus on one aspect of the topic and use details to paint a picture with words.	____	____
3. In my concluding paragraph, I express my feelings about the subject, discuss details that make me feel this way, and reinforce the point of the essay.	____	____
4. I used transitions to connect ideas and create unity in my writing.	____	____
5. I wrote complete sentences that begin with capital letters and used proper end punctuation.	____	____
6. I proofread and edited my composition.	____	____
7. I wrote a corrected copy of my work.	____	____

Submit the completed writing assignment and Practice exercise to your instructor for evaluation.

Composition

This section of the guide provides additional practice in writing a descriptive essay. Choose a fiction or nonfiction selection to read from available book titles. Write a descriptive essay that appeals to the five senses and uses vivid details to create lifelike impressions for the reader. Follow the outline provided in this lesson to write your composition. Use the checklist to help you review and revise your writing.

The Expository Essay

Exposition is writing that gives directions about how to do something or how to get somewhere, explains how something works, or how something happens. The basic structure of the expository essay is chronological because a process usually involves a series of events or steps that must occur in a certain order.

Expository essays use transitions as markers to each step or stage in the process. Transitions like "first," "second," and "third" can be added to the beginnings of sentences or paragraphs to identify each step in the process. Transitions like "before," "after," or "sometimes" can be used to show time relationships when explaining a process.

Practice

Read each part of the following exercise and answer all **16** questions. In the model essay, the author combines exposition, an explanation of how to do something, with persuasion to make recommendations about caring for yourself when you have a cold.

Have you ever tried to wish away a cold? The common cold, with its accompanying cough, fever, aches and pains, can be effectively treated by you. While you can't cure the common cold, you can minimize your discomfort.

There are three basic steps to follow that will help you feel better faster. First, it is important to stay in bed and get lots of rest. The fact is that the body heals itself while in a state of rest and relaxation. Second, use a vaporizer during the night to moisten the air with steam while you sleep. It is easier to breathe when the air is moist than when it's dry. This is especially true when the weather is cold.

Most important, drink plenty of liquids. Drinking fluids while you are sick helps to flush germs and bacteria out of the body and prevents dehydration, especially if you have a fever. Drink about ten to twelve glasses of liquids daily, preferably fruit juices, herb teas and water. Fresh squeezed lemon juice mixed with honey and hot water works wonders. Sleep, moist air to breathe, and liquids to drink will help to make you well again.

Take time to care for yourself when you have a cold. This way, you will recuperate quickly and get back to those things you enjoy doing. While the common cold is not something you can cure, you will feel better if you follow the steps outlined in this essay.

The Introductory Paragraph

The first sentence of this paragraph asks a question that every reader has had experience with. The rest of the paragraph defines the topic and provides an overview for the essay.

1. What do people try to do when they have a cold?

2. What are some characteristics of the common cold?

3. What process does the author propose to explain?

Development Paragraph One

The first development paragraph presents a plan for treating the common cold. Two steps in the process and supporting facts that explain each step are given. Transitions are used to mark the steps the reader can take to treat a cold.

4. How many steps are suggested to the reader for curing the common cold?

5. What step is recommended first?

6. What fact supports this advice?

7. What is the second recommendation?

8. What fact supports this advice?

Development Paragraph Two

The second development paragraph focuses on the third and most important step in the plan. This paragraph uses more extensive examples to make the point. As a result, one paragraph that included all of the information about the plan would be more difficult to understand. For these reasons, the explanation of the three steps was split into two paragraphs. The concluding sentence summarizes the information presented in both development paragraphs.

9. What is the third step recommended?

10. What two facts are used to explain why this step is most important?

11. How many glasses of liquid should you drink each day while you are ill?

12. What kinds of drinks are suggested?

13. Write the sentence that summarizes what the author has said in his development paragraphs.

The Concluding Paragraph

The concluding paragraph restates and supports the topic of the essay, and draws a conclusion.

14. The first sentence reminds you of the topic and encourages you to take action. What action is recommended?

15. The next sentence offers two reasons why you should follow the author's advice. What are they?

16. The essay ends with a summary statement that draws a conclusion. What is it?

Score the Practice exercise using the Answer Key, and go on to the Composition part of this guide.

Composition

This part of the guide will help you apply what you have learned about writing an expository essay. Write your essay about one of the topics listed below. You may find it helpful to use reference sources to gather some facts about the topic. Follow the outline given to write your composition.

Topics

how a significant discovery was made

my favorite hobby

how bees make honey

how to get a learner's permit to drive

how basketball came about

Outline

I. The Introductory Paragraph

    A. Begin your essay with a statement or a question that gets the reader's attention.

    B. Define the topic and provide an overview.

    C. Be sure your reader knows what process or event you will explain.

II. Development Paragraph One

    A. Let the reader know how you plan to develop your essay, the stages in the process or event.

    B. Discuss the beginning steps or stages in a logical order.

    C. Support these steps or stages with facts and examples.

III. Development Paragraph Two

    A. Discuss the most important step or stage in greater depth.

    B. To do this, use more facts and examples than you did in discussing previous steps.

    C. Summarize the information presented in both development paragraphs.

IV. The Concluding Paragraph

    A. Remind the reader of the topic and encourage a response.

    B. Support the topic of the essay.

    C. Summarize by offering an opinion or drawing a conclusion that reinforces the topic of the essay.

Use this Checklist to help you review and revise your writing. Do this for all drafts and your final copy.

Checklist

1. In my introductory paragraph I appeal to the reader's interest, define the topic, and provide an overview of the process or event I explain. _____ _____

2. My first development paragraph gives the reader a plan for the essay, discusses the beginning steps in a logical order, and supports each step with facts and examples. _____ _____

3. In development paragraph two, I discuss the most important stage, use more facts and examples, and summarize the information presented in both development paragraphs. _____ _____

4. In my concluding paragraph I restate the topic, provide more support for it, encourage a response from the reader, and offer an opinion or draw a conclusion. _____ _____

5. I used transitions to connect ideas and create unity in my writing. _____ _____

6. I proofread and edited my composition. _____ _____

7. I wrote a corrected copy of my work. _____ _____

Submit the completed writing assignment and Practice exercise to your Instructor for evaluation.

Composition

This section of the guide provides additional practice in writing an expository essay. Choose a nonfiction selection to read from available book titles. Write an expository essay that gives directions about how to do something or how to get somewhere, explains how something works, or how something happens. Follow the outline provided in this lesson to write your composition. Use the checklist to help you review and revise your writing.

The Persuasive Essay

This guide will help you to understand how a persuasive essay is written. Persuasive writing appeals to your ability to reason and to your emotions. This approach attempts to make the reader think, feel, and even act in a certain way. Persuasion is usually successful when the writer provides good reasons for doing, or not doing, something. Writing persuasively will convince the reader to see things **your** way.

In writing a persuasive essay, it is important to identify four elements of the situation you are writing about. These elements are defined here by the acronym, *PASS*.

Purpose—why you are writing

Audience—to whom you are writing

Subject—the topic of the essay

Status of writer—who you are

Persuasive writing can take the form of an essay, a letter, or a memorandum (memo). **The same content can be presented in any of these forms; only the headings change.** The heading of an essay tells you its title and author. Essay form is most often used by students. The business letter format is used to write a formal message. The memo is used when communicating within the same organization. The memo is less formal than the letter, and conveys less information in the heading. The memo assumes that people know one another.

Practice

Read each part of the following exercise and answer all **15** questions. The model essay takes the form of a memo. The author, an employee of the firm, attempts to convince the Director of Personnel to implement a stress management program for company employees. He does this by offering reasons why such a program would be beneficial to all.

October 24, 1990

To: Maria Arias,
          Director of Personnel

From: Jim Kennedy,
          Sales Manager

Subject: Stress management program for employees

As an employee of this company, I would like to suggest that the Personnel Department offer a program in stress management. Many corporations offer this training to their workers as a means of improving productivity and reducing absenteeism. I believe such a program would benefit our company and its employees.

If our company were to implement a stress management program, I am certain one result would be greater productivity. One out of every five of the Fortune 500 companies now have some kind of stress management program. Many firms realize that too much stress makes workers inefficient. Pressure improves performance to a point, after which efficiency drops off sharply. Learning how to relax and manage stress can actually improve the productivity of employees.

Linked to the need to improve performance and productivity is the need to reduce absenteeism and medical costs. Stress is known to be a major contributor, either directly or indirectly, to heart disease, cancer, lung ailments, accidents, and suicide. By encouraging workers to reduce the strain on their bodies and minds, some companies have been able to make significant reductions in the incidence of stress-related diseases among their employees. Stress management has led to lower medical costs and fewer work hours lost due to absenteeism.

Stress management programs are very popular because they make good business sense. Our firm can have healthier, happier, more productive employees and higher profits. I hope that your department will consider my suggestion and implement a program to combat stress.

Use the model essay to answer the questions below.

The Introductory Paragraph

1. Write a sentence that states the author's purpose.

   _____

2. The writer's audience is:

   _____

3. Indicate the subject of the essay.

   _____

4. Refer to the status of the writer.

   _____

5. What **two** reasons does the author give in support of his suggestion?

   _____

6. Write the sentence that expresses the author's opinion.

   _____

Development Paragraph One

In a persuasive essay, **each** development paragraph explains **one reason** for the author's opinion.

7. Write the topic sentence that states the first reason in support of the author's opinion.

   _____

8. Write the **number** of sentences which help to explain this first reason. _____

9. Write the sentence which restates the topic and concludes this paragraph.

_____

Development Paragraph Two

10. Write the topic sentence that states the second reason in support of the author's opinion.

_____

11. Write the **number** of sentences which help to explain the second reason. _____

12. Write the sentence which restates the topic and concludes this paragraph.

_____

The Concluding Paragraph

13. Write the sentence that restates the topic of the essay.

_____

14. Write a sentence that supports this restatement.

_____

15. Write the sentence that summarizes the author's opinion and concludes the essay.

_____

Score the Practice exercise using the Answer Key, and go on to the Composition part of this guide.

Composition

This part of the guide will help you to write a persuasive essay. Respond to **one** of the four situations presented below with a persuasive composition. You may choose to write this as an essay or a memo. Follow the outline on the next page as you write.

Situations

1. Purpose: To persuade your legislator to vote for or against a law which prohibits smoking in the dining area of restaurants.

   Audience: Your legislator.

   Subject: Smoking in the dining area of restaurants.

   Status of writer: Identify yourself as the writer.

2. Purpose: As a member of the local Board of Education, persuade your colleagues to your position regarding sex education in the schools.

   Audience: Your local Board of Education.

   Subject: Sex education in the schools.

   Status of writer: Identify yourself as the writer.

3. Purpose: To persuade a friend, relative, or colleague to lend you one thousand dollars.

   Audience: A specific individual.

   Subject: A $1,000 loan.

   Status of writer: Identify yourself as the writer.

4. Purpose: To persuade readers of a newspaper or magazine to your point of view regarding the death penalty (Letters to the Editor).

    Audience: Readers of a newspaper or magazine.

    Subject: The death penalty.

    Status of writer: Identify yourself as the writer.

Outline

I. The Introductory Paragraph

   A. In your opening sentence(s), introduce your purpose, audience, subject, and your status as writer. This information can be presented in any order.

   B. State two reasons that support your persuasive argument, but do not explain them here.

   C. Express your opinion and conclude the paragraph.

II. Development Paragraph One

   A. Write a topic sentence that states the first reason in support of your argument.

   B. Write several sentences which explain this reason. Be specific and use details.

   C. Restate the topic of this paragraph and write a conclusion.

III. Development Paragraph Two

   A. Write a topic sentence that states the second reason in support of your argument.

   B. Write several sentences which explain this reason. Be specific and use details.

   C. Restate the topic of this paragraph and write a conclusion.

IV. The Concluding Paragraph

    A. Restate the subject of the essay.

    B. Support this restatement in a sentence or two.

    C. Summarize your opinion and conclude the essay.

Use the Checklist to help you review and revise your writing. Do this for all drafts and your final copy.

Checklist   Yes No

1. In my opening sentence(s) I introduce my purpose, audience, subject, and my status as writer (PASS).   _____ _____

2. In my first paragraph, I state two reasons that support my argument. I express my opinion and conclude the paragraph.   _____ _____

3. Each of my development paragraphs introduce and explain one reason in support of my argument.   _____ _____

4. In my concluding paragraph I restate the subject of the essay, support it, express my opinion, and conclude the essay.   _____ _____

5. I used transitions to connect ideas and create unity in my writing.   _____ _____

6. I proofread and edited my composition.   _____ _____

7. I wrote a corrected copy of my work.   _____ _____

Submit the completed writing assignment and Practice exercise to your instructor for evaluation.

Composition

This section of the guide provides additional practice in writing a persuasive essay. While the expository essay presents facts and examples with little interpretation, the persuasive essay offers facts and opinions in order to directly influence the reader.

Persuasion is often used in writing to the editor of a newspaper or magazine, and in contacting school, college, or public officials. It can also be effective in personal communication with a friend, relative, colleague, or supervisor. In many occupations, the ability to write persuasively can be a major asset. Persuasion is the primary focus of writing in the advertising industry.

Write a persuasive essay for **one** of the four situations presented here. Use the outline provided to do this. Before you write, identify the four elements of your situation: **P**urpose, **A**udience, **S**ubject, and **S**tatus of writer.

Situations

- Write a letter to the editor of a newspaper or magazine about an issue of your choice.

- Write a letter to a school, college, or public official making a request, or offering your opinion about an issue.

- Write an advertisement in the form of a persuasive essay for a product you are selling.

- Write a personal letter of persuasion to a friend, relative, colleague, or supervisor.

Outline

I. The Introductory Paragraph

    A. In your opening sentence(s), introduce your purpose, audience, subject, and your status as writer. This information can be presented in any order.

    B. State two reasons that support your persuasive argument, but do not explain them here.

    C. Express your opinion and conclude the paragraph.

II. Development Paragraph One

    A. Write a topic sentence that states the first reason in support of your argument.

    B. Write several sentences which explain this reason. Be specific and use details.

    C. Restate the topic of this paragraph and write a conclusion.

III. Development Paragraph Two

    A. Write a topic sentence that states the second reason in support of your argument.

    B. Write several sentences which explain this reason. Be specific and use details.

    C. Restate the topic of this paragraph and write a conclusion.

IV. The Concluding Paragraph

    A. Restate the subject of the essay.

    B. Support this restatement in a sentence or two.

    C. Summarize your opinion and conclude the essay.

Use the Checklist to help you review and revise your writing. Do this for all drafts and your final copy.

The Short Report

This guide will help you to understand how a short report is written. Knowing how to write a report is essential in school and useful in many occupations. The short report is organized into three or more paragraphs. The information you use in writing the report will most likely come from one or more of the following sources:

- newspaper and magazine articles

- movies and television shows

- concerts and lectures

- biographies of famous people

- reference books containing information about places and events: past, present, or future

Practice

Read each part of the following exercise and answer all **34** questions. The model report in this guide appeared as an article in a local newspaper. The author of the report included the map on the next page to help define the subject for the reader.

MYSTERIES OF THE BERMUDA TRIANGLE

by Susan Chan

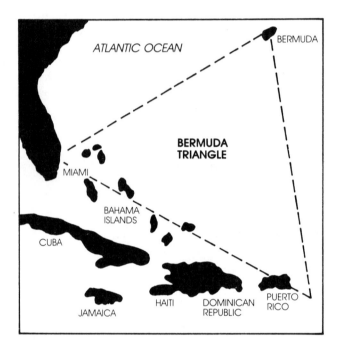

As science editor of this newspaper, it was with great interest that I attended the recent lecture presented by Charles Berlitz, author of *The Bermuda Triangle*. Mr. Berlitz talked about many of the strange and unexplained mysteries that have occurred in the Triangle. The Bermuda or Devil's Triangle is an imaginary area located off the Atlantic coast of the United States (see map). The three points of the triangle are Bermuda, southern Florida, and Puerto Rico. More than 100 planes and ships have vanished, and more than 1,000 lives have been lost in this area. Although there have been extensive searches, not one body or piece of wreckage has ever been found.

Mr. Berlitz spoke of the most well known case, the disappearance of five Navy Avenger bombers and their crews on December 5, 1945. The fourteen men were on a routine training mission off the coast of Florida. The pilots, all expert flyers, reported that every gyro and magnetic compass was "going crazy." The flight leader told the tower that they could not see land, the ocean looked strange, and that they were completely lost. An intensive search for the aircraft and crews produced no life rafts and no wreckage or oil slicks. The National Board of Inquiry said, "They vanished completely as if they had flown to Mars."

Another mystery of the sea was the disappearance of the Navy Supply Ship, U.S.S. Cyclops. The ship with a crew of 309 disappeared on March 4, 1918, in good weather. No radio messages were ever received from the ship and no wreckage was ever found. These unsolved mysteries are among hundreds that puzzle scientists and defy the laws of nature.

Many theories have been offered in an attempt to explain these unusual occurrences in the Bermuda Triangle. Some believe that there is a time-space warp leading to another dimension. Others say that electromagnetic force fields cause planes to crash and ships to be swallowed by the sea. A popular explanation is that UFOs from inner or outer space have kidnapped these vessels and their crews. Whatever the explanation, these disappearances continue to occur today. If you find this topic interesting, you will want to read Charles Berlitz's books, *The Bermuda Triangle* and *Mysteries from Forgotten Worlds*.

The science editor wrote her report based on notes she took at a lecture about the Bermuda Triangle. While she took many notes, she used only those included in the list below. Her notes are presented here without paragraphs and out of order. In the correct order, this information is an outline of the model report.

BERLITZ LECTURE NOTES

National Board of Inquiry said of bombers, "They vanished completely as if they had flown to Mars."

Over 100 planes and ships vanished thus far

Time-space warp leading to other dimensions

Pilots, expert flyers, on training mission, Florida, Dec. 5, 1945

Bermuda Triangle also known as Devil's Triangle

Navy Supply Ship U.S.S. Cyclops with crew of 309 vanished in good weather, March 4, 1918

Flight leader to tower: "Can't see land, ocean looks strange, we're completely lost."

No bodies or wreckage from any disappearances ever found

UFOs from inner or outer space kidnap vessels

Points of triangle: Bermuda, southern Florida, Puerto Rico

Electromagnetic force fields

Imaginary area off southern Atlantic coast of U.S.

Best known disappearance—five Navy Avenger bombers

More than 1,000 lives lost thus far

Search produces no life rafts, no plane wrecks, no oil slicks

Pilots report gyro and magnetic compasses "going crazy"

No radio messages, no wreckage of ship found

The first step in organizing this information is to **group** the notes by heading (topic). Do this by sorting each note into one of four groups. Refer to the model report to help you do this.

Grouping Notes

The Disappearance of Planes (six notes, order not important)

1. _____
2. _____
3. _____
4. _____
5. _____
6. _____

The Bermuda Triangle—What and Where (six notes, order not important)

7. _____
8. _____
9. _____
10. _____
11. _____
12. _____

Explanations and Theories (three notes, order not important)

13. _____
14. _____
15. _____

The Disappearance of Ships (two notes, order not important)

16. _____
17. _____

After you have grouped the notes, there are two steps to **ordering** them. First, the headings are ordered as they appear in the model. This has been done for you. Second, place the notes in the order in which they appear in the model report.

Ordering Notes

I. **The Introductory Paragraph:** The Bermuda Triangle—What and Where (six notes in correct order)

18. _____

19. _____

20. _____

21. _____

22. _____

23. _____

II. **Development Paragraph One:** The Disappearance of Planes (six notes in correct order)

24. _____

25. _____

26. _____

27. _____

28. _____

29. _____

III. **Development Paragraph Two:** The Disappearance of Ships (two notes in correct order)

30. _____

31. _____

IV. **The Concluding Paragraph:** Explanations and Theories (three notes in correct order)

32. _____

33. _____

34. _____

**Score the Practice exercise using the Answer Key, and go
on to the Composition part of this guide.**

Composition

This part of the guide will help you to write a short report.
Three preparatory steps in writing the short report are:

- taking notes
- grouping notes
- ordering notes

You do not have to take your own notes for this exercise. Five
sets of notes are provided for you, each based on a different
topic. For each topic, you are given the reason you are writing
this report and the sources of your information. Choose **one** of
the five topics presented in this section of the guide. Use the
outlines which follow to group and order your notes, and to
write your report.

Topics

The Beatles

The California Gold Rush

Amelia Earhart

Martin Luther King, Jr.

Pablo Picasso

The Beatles

Situation

You are doing a short report on the Beatles, a musical group that rose to fame in the sixties. You have located newspaper and magazine articles about the Beatles and have taken the following notes to use in writing your report.

NOTES

56,000 at Shea Stadium, summer '65, largest concert crowd

Combination of their four personalities and talents unbeatable

John Lennon, Beatles' guiding spirit, came across as most intelligent of Beatles

Known as John, Paul, George, and Ringo to fans

Four scruffy boys from Liverpool would one day set tone for an entire generation

February 1964, on Ed Sullivan show, 70 million watch

Group discovered while playing rock 'n' roll clubs in Liverpool, England

George Harrison most handsome, most dedicated musician

Beatles wrote and recorded many songs

Nobody ever matched this record of hits—mentioned in The Guiness Book of World Records

Largest television audience ever for an entertainment program

Beatles drew large crowds wherever they went on tour

Their music as popular today as when they began

In one week, top five hits on singles charts and top two albums, all by Beatles

Ringo Starr, drummer, most down to earth of Beatles

Paul McCartney, hardest worker, most romantic image

The California Gold Rush

Situation

You are writing a feature article for your school newspaper about the California Gold Rush. On a visit to Sutter's Mill, site of the first discovery, you collected books and materials for your report. You took the notes below from these sources and will use them to write a three paragraph report.

NOTES

Stood waist-deep in icy streams for days, found little gold

Presence of settlers led to growth of agriculture, commerce, transportation, and industry

People even going on crutches and stretchers

Before 1848, California sparsely populated

California now most populated state in Union

Claim jumpers: thieves who stole miners' gold and rights to their claims

California Gold Rush of 1849, America's first great migration

Thousands of people from all over the world flocked to gold fields

A few struck it rich, most miners suffered

Miners came to California, stayed to make a great state out of the land

Husbands left wives, sons left mothers, sailors left their ships

Successful miners attacked by claim jumpers

Discovery of gold at Sutter's Mill early in 1848 brought 40,000 prospectors to California

Amelia Earhart

Situation

As part of a course which is studying women in history, you have attended a documentary film at a museum. You have been asked to write a short report based on the notes you took on the film and from a biography of Amelia Earhart.

NOTES

As young girl, loved "boys" sports and games

Presented with medals by many cities: Chicago, New York, Philadelphia, Los Angeles, and Mexico City

Awarded the French Legion of Honor in Paris

August, 1932, set women's non-stop transcontinental speed record in flight from California to New Jersey

Born in Atchison, Kansas, July 24, 1898

Lost over Pacific during flight around world, July 3, 1937

Was reported that Earhart and copilot Noonan crash-landed plane in South Pacific and executed as spies by Japanese

First woman pilot to fly from Honolulu to California, 1935

Awarded Distinguished Flying Cross by United States Congress

Famous worldwide—paved the way for other female pilots

Her disappearance never adequately explained

Married George Putnam, publisher and author, who encouraged Amelia in her career

One of America's greatest heroines

Flies the Atlantic solo, in 14 hours, 56 minutes, May 21, 1932

Flights gain fame and fortune for Amelia almost overnight

Fragment of wood found with writing: "To my husband—I have crashed near Hawaii—sharks all around, A.E."

Foreign countries honor her: Mexico, France, Belgium, and England

Gold medal of the National Geographic Society presented to her by President Herbert Hoover, 1932

Martin Luther King, Jr.

Situation

You have chosen to write a short biography of a famous person as part of a course project. You took the following notes from two books about Martin Luther King, Jr.

NOTES

Organized massive civil rights March on Washington in 1963

Married Coretta Scott King in 1953, had four children

1963 designated "Man of the Year" by *Time* magazine

In Memphis, killed by assassin's bullet, April 4, 1968

World-famous leader who fought racial discrimination and prejudice

Nonviolent principles derived from Indian leader Mahatma Gandhi

Born in Atlanta, Georgia on January 15, 1929

Received Ph.D. in Theology, 1955

Plans for "Poor People's March on Washington" interrupted by trip to Memphis, Tennessee to support striking sanitation workers

Known for nonviolent philosophy in seeking social change

Baptist minister in Montgomery, Alabama, 1954-1960

Organized yearlong boycott against segregated city bus lines in Montgomery, 1955

1964, awarded Nobel Peace Prize—youngest Peace Laureate in history

Graduated from Morehouse College in 1948 with honors, 19 years old

Always supporting working man's struggle

During '63 March on Washington, King delivered his famous speech, "I Have a Dream"

Pablo Picasso

Situation

A local art magazine is sponsoring a contest for the best short
biographical sketch of a famous 20th century artist. The winner
will receive a $100 gift certificate for books and art supplies.
You took the following notes from an encyclopedia and two
books on Pablo Picasso.

NOTES

From age of seven, never without pencil in hand

Born in Malaga, Spain, October 25, 1881

His blue period depicted life of the poor

Work can be viewed in terms of both color and style

In early years, 1901 to 1908, painted first in shades of blue, and later in rose

Illustration, facing page, shows later cubist style; picture of Picasso is in foreground

Died in 1973 at age of 92

Picasso said, "To draw you must close your eyes and sing."

At age 15, admitted to well known art school by completing project in one day which took most students a month

Don Jose, his father, a painter and art teacher

Picasso painted in many styles, but cubism most important

Picasso paints famous cubist mural, "Guernica" to express his feelings about bombing of Spanish town during Civil War, 1937

He will always be considered one of the greatest artists of all time

Lived most of his adult life in France

During rose period, painted many circus people who were his friends and models

"The Old Guitarist" painted during blue period, on display in Art Institute of Chicago

First phase of cubism, 1907 to 1912, shows all dimensions of an object: width, height, and depth

Later phase of cubism, after 1912, shows objects and people in two dimensions, flat, without depth

First, study the notes for your topic and group them into categories (headings) that you create.

Grouping Notes

Heading: _____

(Number of notes: _____, order not important)

_____

_____

_____

_____

_____

Heading: _____

(Number of notes: _____, order not important)

_____

_____

_____

_____

Heading: _____

(Number of notes: _____, order not important)

_____

_____

_____

_____

Heading: _____

(Number of notes: _____, order not important)

_____

_____

_____

_____

Now, organize the notes you have grouped. First, **determine the order of the headings:** introduction, development, and conclusion. This report may have one or more development paragraphs. Next, **order your notes** so that there is meaning and continuity to each sequence.

Ordering Notes

    I. Introductory Paragraph: _____
        (list notes in order)   (heading)

_____

_____

_____

_____

_____

    II. Development Paragraph: _____
        (list notes in order)   (heading)

_____

_____

_____

_____

    III. Development Paragraph: _____
        (list notes in order)   (heading)

_____

_____

_____

_____

    IV. Concluding Paragraph: _____
        (list notes in order)   (heading)

_____

_____

_____

_____

After you have grouped and ordered your notes, follow the Short Report Outline to present the information you have organized.

Outline

I. The Introductory Paragraph

    A. Your opening sentences let the reader know your topic, the audience you are addressing, and your position as the author. This information may be presented in any order.

        Example In the model report on the Bermuda Triangle the author:

           1. states the topic (the Bermuda Triangle).

           2. speaks to her audience (the readers of the article).

           3. tells the reader her status as writer (science editor of the newspaper).

    B. Define the topic: who, what, where, when.

    C. Write a conclusion that leads the reader from the introduction to the development portion of the essay (transition).

II. The Development Paragraph(s)—For each paragraph:

    A. State the topic of **this** paragraph.

    B. Offer specifics: facts, details, and information pertaining to the topic of **this** paragraph.

    C. Briefly summarize the major point of **this** paragraph.

III. The Concluding Paragraph

    A. Bring the reader up to date by referring to the current status of the topic of your report.

    B. Express your personal view with regard to the topic.

    C. Write a conclusion for your report.

Use the Checklist to help you review and revise your writing. Do this for all drafts and your final copy.

Checklist   Yes   No

1. I chose one of five topics provided and grouped the notes into categories (headings) that I created.   _____   _____

2. I organized my headings and notes in a sequence that has meaning and continuity.   _____   _____

3. I followed the Short Report Outline to present information.   _____   _____

4. I used transitions to connect ideas and create unity in my writing.   _____   _____

5. I proofread and edited my report.   _____   _____

6. I wrote a corrected copy of my work.   _____   _____

Submit the completed writing assignment and Practice exercise to your instructor for evaluation.

Composition

This section of the guide provides additional practice in writing a short report. Write a report on the topic of your choice. Your instructor may also suggest topics. Information for your report may come from one or more sources as listed in the very beginning of The Short Report guide.

The three preparatory steps in writing the short report are taking notes, grouping notes, and ordering notes.

Taking Notes

Your notes should define the topic with specific information: who, what, where, when, how, why.

Write your notes on **index cards** according to the steps outlined here. Notes taken initially on notepaper can later be transferred to index cards.

1. Write one note per card.
2. Indicate the source in the upper right hand corner.
3. Write the subject in the center of the card. Your note is written just below this title.
4. If your source is a book, write the page number on which the information appears. Record this in the lower left corner of the card.
5. Write on only one side of the card.

SAMPLE NOTE CARD

The Bermuda Triangle
by Charles Berlitz

Disappearance of Ships

December 1967: Revonoc, all-weather forty-six foot racing yacht; disappeared within sight of land near the Florida Keys.

Page 56

Grouping Notes

In order to group your notes, you need to establish headings. Write each heading on a separate index card and spread these out on a table. Place each note card under the most appropriate heading. Do this until you are satisfied with the way your notes are grouped. Use this procedure for grouping information whenever you take notes for a report.

Ordering Notes

First, arrange the headings in order as they will appear in the report: introduction, development, and conclusion. Next, order the note cards for each heading to give meaning and continuity to each sequence.

When you have completed the three preparatory steps above, you are ready to write your report. Follow the Short Report Outline to present the information you have organized.

Outline

I. The Introductory Paragraph

   A. Your opening sentences let the reader know your topic, the audience you are addressing, and your status as the author. This information may be presented in any order.

   B. Define the topic: who, what, where, when.

   C. Write a conclusion that leads the reader from the introduction to the development portion of the essay (transition).

II. The Development Paragraph(s)—For each paragraph:

    A. State the topic of **this** paragraph.

    B. Offer specifics: facts, details, and information pertaining to the topic of **this** paragraph.

    C. Briefly summarize the major point of **this** paragraph.

III. The Concluding Paragraph

    A. Bring the reader up to date by referring to the current status of the topic of your report.

    B. Express your personal view with regard to the topic.

    C. Write a conclusion for your report.

Use the Checklist to help you review and revise your writing. Do this for all drafts and your final copy.

Checklist   Yes   No

	Yes	No
1. I selected a topic and used one or more sources.	____	____
2. I completed the three preparatory steps for writing a report: taking notes, grouping notes, and ordering notes.	____	____
3. I followed the Short Report Outline to write my report.	____	____
4. I used transitions to connect ideas and create unity in my writing.	____	____
5. I proofread and edited my report	____	____
6. I wrote a corrected copy of my work.	____	____

Submit the completed writing assignment and Practice exercise to your instructor for evaluation.

The Book Report

This guide will help you to write a book report. The report will be based on a novel that you read. A novel creates impressions for the reader through setting, characterization, conflict and plot, as well as theme.

The **setting** tells the reader where and when the story takes place. It also gives relevant background information and creates atmosphere for the story.

Characterization is the creation of imaginary people who are so believable that the reader views them as real. The character's name, physical appearance, actions, words, thoughts, and feelings all contribute to creating this impression. What others say and how they feel about a character gives us additional insight into that character.

Conflict is a struggle between opposing forces. Conflict in literature can take several forms. A character may struggle against another character, against society, against oneself, against nature, or against the unknown. Often, more than one conflict is apparent in the novel. Readers want to know how characters react to conflict and how the story ends.

1. Conflict with others sets one character against another and is the most basic kind of conflict.

2. Conflict with society sets one character against accepted ways of thinking and behaving. Since society is made up of people, this is conflict between people on a larger scale.

3. Conflict with self involves a struggle that takes place within a character. It occurs when an individual is confronted with a difficult choice or an unpleasant situation.

4. Conflict with nature sets a character against the forces of nature.

5. Conflict with the unknown sets a character against that which is beyond human comprehension such as: fate, magic, or death.

The **plot** is a series of events in a novel through which the author reveals what is happening, to whom, and why. The author builds tension through the development of the plot.

Complications are twists and turns in the plot which create tension and further conflict. Every plot is built around conflict in order to create interest and build suspense.

The **climax** is the point of greatest tension in the story. A novel will often have several points of high tension, each followed by a **resolution.** All plots follow a basic pattern like the one shown below in the chart.

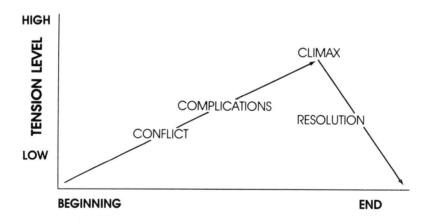

The **theme** of a novel conveys the author's message about people and the world in which we live. One theme may be stated in different ways. One novel may have several themes. The theme is expressed through setting, characterization, and conflict and plot. Themes apply to people in general and can also apply to us personally. Our understanding of the author's message may reinforce, or even change, some of our attitudes and opinions.

Practice

This section of the guide is designed to help you collect and organize information for a book report. Read each part of the following exercise and answer all **13** questions.

1. Write the title of the book.

   _____

2. Write the author's name.

   _____

3. Write one or two sentences that tell what the book is about.

   _____

4. Who is the narrator of the story?

   _____

5. Where does the story take place?

   _____

6. When does the story take place?

   _____

7. Provide background information that is relevant to the story in the novel. _____

8. Which of the five forms of conflict are presented in this novel? A novel, unlike a short story, will often have more than one form of conflict. _____

9. For each of the major characters in the novel (limit to four), give the following information:

   Name _____

   Character's role _____

   Description _____

10. Choose at least **two** scenes that express the major conflict and lead to further complications in the novel. Write the **page number** and the **sentence** that identifies the beginning of each scene.

    Page number _____

    Sentence _____

11. Choose a scene that involves the point of greatest tension. Write the **page number** and **sentence** that identifies the beginning of this scene.

    Page number _____

    Sentence _____

12. How does the novel end? _____

13. What is the author's message in the novel? _____

After you have completed the Practice exercise, go on to the Composition part of this guide.

Composition

This part of the guide will help you to write a book report. Use the material that you have produced in the Practice exercise to write your report. Follow the outline presented here.

Outline

I. The Introductory Paragraph (**setting**)

    A. State the title and author of the book.

    B. Write one or two sentences that summarize what this book is about.

    C. Who is the narrator of the story?

    D. Where and when does the story take place? Provide relevant background information.

    E. Which of the five forms of conflict are presented in this novel?

II. Paragraphs Two through Five (**characterization**)

    A. Write a separate paragraph for each major character in the novel (limit to four). Develop each paragraph in the following way:

        1. Introduce the character by name and tell what role he or she plays in the story.

        2. Describe the character.

        3. What important interactions take place between this character and others in the story?

        4. What words spoken in the story help us to understand this character? Explain.

5. In what way, if any, does the character change by the end of the story?

6. How do you feel about this character, and why?

III. Paragraphs Six through Eight (**conflict and plot**)

    A. Describe **two** scenes that express the major conflict in the book, and show how they lead to further complications. Write a separate paragraph for each scene.

    B. Describe **the scene** that involves the point of greatest tension in the story, and show how it leads to the resolution of the conflict. Write this in paragraph form.

IV. Paragraph Nine (**theme**)

    A. Tell how the novel ends.

    B. What is the author's message?

    C. How does the theme apply to people in general?

    D. How does the theme apply to you personally?

V. Paragraph Ten (**your opinion**)

    A. Tell whether or not you liked this book, and why.

    B. How did the book reinforce, or change, any attitudes or opinions you may have had?

    C. Would you recommend this book to others? Why or why not?

Use the Checklist to help you review and revise your writing. Do this for all drafts and your final copy.

Checklist   Yes   No

1. In my introductory paragraph I state the title and author, summarize the story, and indicate the narrator. I describe the setting and the form(s) of conflict presented in this novel.   _____ _____

2. Paragraphs two through five each describe a major character in the novel, according to the outline.   _____ _____

3. Paragraphs six and seven describe scenes that express the major conflict in the book.   _____ _____

4. Paragraph eight describes a scene that involves the point of greatest tension in the novel.   _____ _____

5. In paragraph nine, I tell how the novel ends and the author's message. I show how the theme applies to people in general and to me personally.   _____ _____

6. In paragraph ten, I tell how I feel about the book.   _____ _____

7. I used transitions to connect ideas and create unity in my writing.   _____ _____

8. I proofread and edited my report.   _____ _____

9. I wrote a corrected copy of my work.   _____ _____

Submit the completed writing assignment and Practice exercise to your instructor for evaluation.

The Research Paper

This guide will help you to understand how to write a research paper. The skills you have acquired in writing the short report are also used in the research paper. While the form of both is the same—introduction, development, conclusion—the research report has more development paragraphs. Knowing how to write a research paper is essential in school and useful in many occupations.

Practice

Read each part of the following exercise and answer all **79** questions. The model research paper explains Transactional Analysis, an interesting theory about human behavior. Note that the model begins with a cover sheet which serves as a title page for the paper.

Transactional Analysis

by

Marcia Thomas

Psychology 101

Mr. David Morse

December 6, 1990

Transactional Analysis (TA) is an exciting and practical way of learning about yourself and how you interact with others. Transactions can take the form of words, gestures, or physical contact. When people communicate with one another, they are involved in a transaction. Analysis explains the transaction and helps us to understand why people are speaking, gesturing, or making physical contact. TA can be used at work, in school, in your personal life, and wherever people interact. This paper will introduce you to some of the main ideas of TA theory and show how they can be useful to you.

Imagine that there are three people inside of you. Each of these people is you, at different times. These three people think for you, feel for you, and act for you. They are not actually people, but three different ways in which you see the world. Dr. Eric Berne called these "Ego (Self) States" and named them the Parent, Adult, and Child (Freed 1976, 4). The Parent in each of us tells us what we're supposed to do, for better or for worse. The Adult is the thinking part of a person, regardless of age. The Child is the feeling self. For any decision that has to be made, the Parent has beliefs about it, the Adult has thoughts about it, and the Child has feelings about it. All three ego states play a part in our view of the world.

The Parent ego state is made up of behavior and attitudes copied from parents and other authority figures. Their messages are carried in our heads "on tape." The Parent can be either critical or nurturing. The Critical Parent is authoritarian,

judgmental, and moralistic. The Nurturing Parent is caring, supportive, and understanding. The Nurturing Parent acts out of concern for others, while the Critical Parent acts out of a need to control (Woollams and Brown 1979, 27). When you help a friend, you're in your Nurturing Parent. If you scold him for asking for help, you're in your Critical Parent.

The Adult ego state is often called the "computer." It collects and stores information and figures out answers to problems. The Adult thinks clearly and makes logical decisions. Of the three ego states, the Adult is the best evaluator of reality because it is not clouded by emotion. The Adult is interested, observant, and evaluative. The Adult can evaluate the emotions and demands of both the Child and Parent ego states. The more you use your Adult, the better it functions. Right now, by reading this page, you are using your Adult to learn.

The Child ego state is the part of us that feels. A person, regardless of age, acting from his Child ego state might be inquisitive, affectionate, selfish, cruel, playful, or manipulative (James and Jongeward 1971, 127). The Child ego state is made up of three parts: the Natural Child, the Little Professor, and the Adapted Child. The Natural Child is really the infant still inside each of us. It is like a self-centered baby who is affectionate when its needs are met and angry when they are not met. The Little Professor, the creative and intuitive part of your Child ego state, builds sandcastles and intuits the meaning of a friend's nod. The

3

Adapted Child seeks the approval of others, especially parent or authority figures. Doing what others ask may lead us to learn about sharing, taking turns, and being sociable. On the other hand, always doing what others ask inevitably leads us to suppress our feelings. The Natural Child, the Little Professor, and the Adapted Child are three different ways that people express their feelings.

If you know which ego state you are in during a transaction—Parent, Adult, or Child—then understanding and getting along with others becomes easier. There are basically four different ways of identifying ego states (Freed, A. and M. 1977, 38). One way is to know how you feel. If you are feeling happy, sad, or angry, your Child is in charge. If you stop feeling because you hear yourself saying, "Don't be unhappy," your Parent is in charge. When you start thinking about why you feel a particular way, the Adult is taking over.

Another way to figure out which ego state you are in is by listening to the words you use. You are in your Parent when you use words like: "Don't. You should. You must. I'll take care of you. You're okay. Have a nice day." You are in your Adult when you use words like: "What? Why? How? I think. Let me check it out." You are in your Child when you use words like: "I want. I don't care. No! I won't. Wow! Yummy! Darn (or worse)."

A third way to know what state you are in is to look at how you are acting. If you are screaming, crying, or daydreaming, you

are in your Child. If you are scolding, helping a friend, or giving an order, you're in your Parent. If you are reading, answering questions, or trying to figure out which ego state is in charge, you're in your Adult.

The fourth way is to be aware of how others are acting toward you. If people are often critical of you, you are probably in your Child with them. Switch to your Adult and see what happens. If you find yourself being critical of others, you probably want and need something. Take the pressure off by doing something pleasurable for yourself. When you do, you'll find yourself in your Natural Child. When you're not feeling good or getting what you want in a situation, switch ego states. Often, making a change leads to more enjoyable and meaningful transactions.

Every transaction involves an exchange of strokes. A stroke is any act by someone else that lets you know they are there. It may be a look, a word, or a touch. Strokes can be positive or negative. Positive strokes include compliments, smiles, encouragement, and touching that feels good (hugs). Negative strokes include put-downs, criticism, teasing, and touching that feels bad (slaps). We all need strokes to survive. Infants who do not experience enough touch suffer mentally and physically, and may even die as a result of stroke deprivation (Spitz 1945, 53). Although we prefer positive strokes, people will take negative strokes over nothing at all.

5

People's hunger for strokes often leads them to get strokes any way they can. Some straightforward ways of getting strokes are by working, having fun, and being close to others. Crooked ways of getting strokes involve playing psychological games. Games are ways of getting strokes when we don't think we can get them any other way. We've got to con or trick people into giving us strokes. "See what you made me do" is the first line of a game in which you blame others for your mistakes. In this way you collect anger strokes for being one up on others. "Poor Me" is a game in which you complain to others about your situation. In this way you collect sympathy strokes for being one down to others. "If you find yourself going through a similar set of behaviors with the same or different people, and things always wind up badly for you, maybe you're playing a game. Most of us do until we learn how to quit and come on straight" (Freed 51).

Now that you have been introduced to Transactional Analysis, try applying what you have learned. When you are feeling bad or not getting what you want from transactions with others, change the outcome by switching to another ego state. You'll notice that the strokes you get from honest transactions feel much better than those you get by playing games. When we give up the need to be one up or one down to others, we can all be winners.

BIBLIOGRAPHY

Freed, Alvyn. 1976. *T. A. for Teens*. California: Jalmar Press.

Freed, Alvyn and Margaret. 1977. *T. A. for Kids*. California: Jalmar Press.

James, Muriel and Dorothy Jongeward. 1971. *Born to Win*. Philippines: Addison-Wesley Publishing Company, Inc.

Spitz, Renee. 1945. "Hospitalism: Genesis of Psychiatric Conditions in Early Childhood," *Psychoanalytic Study of the Child*. 1: 53-74.

Woollams, Stan and Michael Brown. 1979. *The Total Handbook of Transactional Analysis*. New Jersey: Prentice-Hall, Inc.

The model paper you have just read has twelve paragraphs. The list below contains the twelve paragraph headings out of their proper sequence. Arrange these headings in the same order as the paragraphs appear in the model. Use the outline on the next page to help you do this.

Paragraph Headings

Exchange of Strokes: Positive and Negative

Applying What You Have Learned

Transactional Analysis Defined

Three People Inside of You: Parent, Adult, Child

Know Your Ego State: Your Feelings

Hunger for Strokes: Games

Parent Ego State Defined

Know Your Ego State: Your Actions

Know Your Ego State: Other's Reactions to You

Adult Ego State Defined

Know Your Ego State: Your Words

Child Ego State Defined

The **introduction** to the model report is completed in one paragraph. Place the heading for the first paragraph next to the words *The Introduction* in the outline.

The **development** portion of the paper contains ten paragraphs (A-J). Place the heading for each paragraph in correct sequence.

The **conclusion** of the report is presented in one paragraph. Place the heading for the last paragraph next to the words *The Conclusion* in the outline.

Outline for Ordering Paragraph Headings

1.   I. The Introduction _____

       II. The Development

2.   A. _____

3.   B. _____

4.   C. _____

5.   D. _____

6.   E. _____

7.   F. _____

8.   G. _____

9.   H. _____

10.   I. _____

11.   J. _____

12.   III. The Conclusion _____

In the exercise that follows, the paragraph headings of the model research paper are presented in order. The notes for each paragraph are out of sequence. Order the notes as they appear in the report.

Order the notes within each set as they appear in each paragraph. Write the number 1 next to the first note in a paragraph, the number 2 next to the second note, and so on. The first set has been placed in the correct order for you. Do the same for the remaining sets of notes.

Transactional Analysis Defined

13. __3__ analysis: explains the transaction

14. __4__ TA useful wherever people interact

15. __1__ exciting and practical way to learn about yourself, others

16. __2__ transactions: words, gestures, physical contact

Three People Inside You: Parent, Adult, Child

17. _____ Child—the feeling self

18. _____ Parent—tells us what to do

19. _____ Dr. Eric Berne's Ego States: Parent, Adult, Child

20. _____ Adult—thinking part of person

21. _____ three *people* think, feel, and act for you

22. _____ ego states shape our view of world

Parent Ego State Defined

23. _____ Critical Parent: authoritarian, judgmental, moralistic

24. _____ messages in our heads *on tape*

25. _____ concern for vs. control of others

26. _____ Parent ego state copies authority figures

27. _____ Nurturing Parent: caring, supportive, understanding

Adult Ego State Defined

28. _____ Adult thinks clearly, makes logical decisions

29. _____ Adult ego state best evaluator of reality

30. _____ the more you use Adult, the better it functions

31. _____ Adult evaluates both Child and Parent ego states

32. _____ Adult ego state like a computer

Child Ego State Defined

33. _____ Child: Natural Child, Little Professor, Adapted Child

34. _____ doing what others ask—sharing and being social

35. _____ Adapted Child—seeks approval of others

36. _____ three different ways people express feelings

37. _____ Child ego state *feels*

38. _____ Child ego state, regardless of age, can be inquisitive, affectionate, selfish, cruel, playful, manipulative

39. _____ Natural Child—infant still within us

40. _____ always doing what others ask—suppressing feelings

41. _____ Little Professor—creative and intuitive

Know Your Ego State: Your Feelings

42. _____ happy, sad, angry—Child in charge

43. _____ *Don't*—Parent in charge

44. _____ knowing which ego state you're in—Parent, Adult, Child

45. _____ know how you feel

46. _____ why you feel that way—Adult taking over

47. _____ four different ways to identify ego states

Know Your Ego State: Your Words

48. _____ Adult words: *What, Why, How, I think*

49. _____ listen to your words

50. _____ Child words: *I want, I don't care, Wow!, Darn!*

51. _____ Parent words: *Don't, You should, I'll take care of you*

Know Your Ego State: Your Actions

52. _____ figuring out which ego state is in charge—Adult

53. _____ reading, asking or answering questions—Adult

54. _____ look at how you are acting

55. _____ screaming, crying, daydreaming—Child

56. _____ scolding, helping, ordering—Parent

Know Your Ego State: Others' Reactions

57. _____ get into your Natural Child

58. _____ switching ego states leads to more meaningful transactions

59. _____ if people critical of you, you're probably in Child

60. _____ be aware of others' actions toward you

61. _____ if you're critical of others, you probably need something

Exchange of Strokes: Positive and Negative

62. _____ strokes are necessary for survival

63. _____ negative strokes: criticism, teasing, slaps

64. _____ negative strokes better than no strokes at all

65. _____ transaction involves exchange of strokes

66. _____ strokes are recognition: a look, a word, a touch

67. _____ positive strokes: compliments, smiles, hugs

68. _____ strokes can be positive or negative

69. _____ positive strokes are preferred

70. _____ infants deprived of touch suffer mentally, physically, and may even die

Hunger for Strokes: Games

71. _____ getting crooked strokes—playing psychological games

72. _____ *Poor me*—complaining to collect sympathy strokes

73. _____ getting straightforward strokes: working, having fun, being close to others

74. _____ "If you find yourself going through a similar set of behaviors with the same or different people, and things always wind up badly for you, maybe you're playing a game. Most of us do until we learn how to quit and come on straight."

75. _____ people hunger for strokes

Applying What You Have Learned

76. _____ strokes from honest transactions feel better

77. _____ feeling bad, switch to another ego state

78. _____ we can all be winners

79. _____ try applying what you've learned

Score the Practice exercise using the Answer Key, and go on to the Composition part of this guide.

Composition

This part of the guide will help you to write a research paper. In order to write a good paper, it is important to be organized. The following notes spell out, in detail, the steps to take in writing a research report.

Selecting a Topic

There are many ways to choose a topic. You may already have one in mind. Your instructor may offer suggestions. You can also use *The Subject Guide to Books in Print* or other reference sources.

One way of choosing a topic is to make a list of the subjects that interest you. Next to each, write those ideas that occur to you in relation to the subject. See the example below. Your ideas will lead you to a topic for your research report.

Subject (general)	**Ideas** (specific)
Antiques	weapons, toys, cars, clothes
Energy	solar, nuclear, geothermal, psychic
Geography	Hawaii, Puerto Rico, Himalayas, Amazon River
Famous performers	Michael Jackson, Marilyn Monroe, Clint Eastwood, Diana Ross
Inventions	the lightbulb, the wheel, the telephone, the computer

Organizing Your Information

Once you have decided on a topic, use the library's resources for gathering information and taking notes.

1. take notes on index cards
2. determine paragraph headings
3. group notes by heading
4. order headings as they will appear in report
5. order notes under each heading

Writing the Paper

When you have selected a topic, taken notes, grouped your notes and ordered them, you are ready to write your report. Follow the Research Paper Outline to present the information you have organized.

Outline

I. The Introductory Paragraph

   A. Begin with a strong statement or question that appeals to the reader's interest.

   B. Define the topic for your audience: who, what, where, when, how.

   C. State a plan of development for the report and provide a transition to the next paragraph.

II. The Development Paragraphs: For each paragraph:

   A. State the topic of **this** paragraph.

   B. Offer specifics: facts, details, explanations, and information pertaining to the topic of **this** paragraph.

   C. Briefly summarize the major point of **this** paragraph.

III. The Concluding Paragraph

    A. Bring the reader up to date by referring to the current status of the topic of your report.

    B. Express your personal view with regard to the topic.

    C. Write a conclusion for your report.

IV. Documentation

    A. In the body of your paper, each reference that appears in parentheses follows the same "author-date" system. This parenthetical reference includes the author's last name, the work's year of publication, and the number of the page on which the author's specific quote or ideas appear, e.g. (Freed 1976, 4). When referring to a source which has already been noted, you need only write the author's name and page number in parenthesis, e.g. (Freed 51).

    B. The bibliography page lists the books you used in doing the research paper. This list is alphabetized by author's name. Each citation also includes the year and title of publication, as well as the name of the publisher. Citations for journal articles include the name of the magazine in which the article appears. The *MLA Handbook for Writers of Research Papers*, published by the Modern Language Association of America, is a complete guide to writing the research paper.

Use the Checklist to help you review and revise your writing. Do this for all drafts and your final copy. Type your research paper on unlined bond paper. Double-space and use only one side of the page.

Checklist   Yes   No

1. I selected a topic, took notes, grouped my notes and ordered them.   ____ ____

2. I followed the Research Paper Outline to write my report.   ____ ____

3. I used the correct form for author-date references.   ____ ____

4. I documented my sources in a Bibliography.   ____ ____

5. I used transitions to connect ideas and create unity in my writing.   ____ ____

6. I proofread and edited my research paper.   ____ ____

7. I typed a corrected copy of my work.   ____ ____

Submit the completed writing assignment and Practice exercise to your instructor for evaluation.

Answer Key

Business Letter: Employment

1. a	5. d	9. B	13. A
2. b	6. b	10. A	14. C
3. b	7. C	11. C	15. B
4. a	8. A	12. B	

16. why you are writing

17. the position applied for

18. how you heard of the opening

19. qualifications to do this work

20. reasons for wanting this job

21. relevant career goals

22. reference to enclosed resume

23. request for an interview

24. how you can be reached

Business Letter: Ordering

1. street address	12. state	23. comma
2. state	13. greeting	24. lower case letter
3. capital letters	14. Dear Sir or Madam	25. sign
4. comma	15. : colon	26. signature
5. zip code	16. body	27. B
6. date	17. explains	28. A
7. year	18. two	29. A
8. day	19. product	30. A
9. inside address	20. cost	31. B
10. name	21. sent	32. B
11. cities	22. closing	

33. indicate the product you are ordering

34. brief description of product, including model or reference number

35. special instructions, if any

36. how you plan to pay for merchandise

37. reference to postage and handling

38. how you would like product shipped

Business Letter: Complaint

1. A	7. date you ordered product
2. B	8. description of product and model number
3. B	9. cost of product, including shipping
4. B	10. date you received product
5. A	11. description of product received
6. A	12. what you want seller to do

The Narrative Essay

1. in a little restaurant

2. a couple in their late thirties

3. a long, upholstered bench built into a wall

4. sitting opposite the couple

5. first person narrative/the narrator is a character in the story

6. having dinner

7. it is the husband's birthday and the wife has planned a surprise for him

8. a small birthday cake

9. they played "Happy Birthday to You"

10. she beamed with pride

11. they tried to help out with applause

12. he was embarrassed and indignant

13. expressing anger that is not justified

14. "Oh, now, don't be like that!"

15. some punishing thing, quick and curt and unkind

16. she couldn't bear to look at the woman, so she stared at her plate for a long time

17. she was crying quietly and heartbrokenly and hopelessly

18. any answer is correct

The Descriptive Essay

1. taste	10. sight	19. touch	28. sight
2. sight	11. sound	20. taste	29. sound
3. touch	12. sound	21. sight	30. sound
4. touch	13. taste	22. sight	31. sight & sound
5. smell	14. sound	23. taste	32. sight
6. sight	15. sight	24. touch	33. taste
7. sight	16. taste	25. sight & sound	34. sound
8. sound	17. sight	26. sight & sound	35. sight
9. sound	18. sight	27. touch	36. touch

The Expository Essay

1. wish it away
2. cough, fever, aches, pains
3. how to minimize the discomforts of a cold
4. three steps
5. stay in bed and get lots of rest
6. the body heals itself while in a state of rest and relaxation
7. use a vaporizer to moisten the air with steam while you sleep
8. it is easier to breath when the air is moist, especially in cold weather
9. drink plenty of liquids
10. a. fluids help to flush germs and bacteria out of the body
    b. fluids prevent dehydration, especially if you have a fever

11. ten to twelve glasses of liquid

12. lemon and other fruit juices, hot water, herb teas

13. Sleep, moist air to breathe, and liquids to drink will help to make you well again.

14. take time to care for yourself

15. a. you will recuperate quickly

    b. you get back to those things you enjoy doing

16. While the common cold is not something you can cure, you will feel better if you follow the steps outlined in this essay.

The Persuasive Essay

1. As an employee of this company, I would like to suggest that the Personnel Department offer a program in stress management.

2. Maria Arias, Director of Personnel

3. a stress management program for employees

4. Jim Kennedy, Sales Manager

5. improved productivity; reduced absenteeism

6. I believe such a program would benefit our company and its employees.

7. If our company were to implement a stress management program, I am certain one result would be greater productivity.

8. three

9. Learning how to relax and manage stress can actually improve the productivity of employees.

10. Linked to the need to improve performance and productivity is the need to reduce absenteeism and medical costs.

11. two

12. Stress management has led to lower medical costs and fewer work hours lost due to absenteeism.

13. Stress management programs are very popular because they make good business sense.

14. Our firm can have healthier, happier, more productive employees and higher profits.

15. I hope that your department will consider my suggestion and implement a program to combat stress.

The Short Report

1. National Board of Inquiry said of bombers, "They vanished completely as if they had flown to Mars."

2. pilots, expert flyers, on training mission, Florida, Dec. 5, 1945

3. flight leader to tower: "Can't see land, ocean looks strange, we're completely lost."

4. best known disappearance—five Navy Avenger bombers

5. search produces no life rafts, no plane wrecks, no oil slicks

6. pilots report gyro and magnetic compasses "going crazy"

7. over 100 planes and ships vanished thus far

8. Bermuda Triangle also known as Devil's Triangle

9. no bodies or wreckage from any disappearance ever found

10. points of triangle: Bermuda, southern Florida, Puerto Rico

11. imaginary area off southern Atlantic coast of U.S.

12. more than 1,000 lives lost thus far

13. time-space warp leading to other dimensions

14. UFOs from inner or outer space kidnap vessels

15. electromagnetic force fields

16. Navy supply ship U.S.S. Cyclops with crew of 309 vanished in good weather, March 4, 1918

17. no radio messages, no wreckage of ship found

18. Bermuda Triangle also known as Devil's Triangle

19. imaginary area off southern Atlantic coast of U.S.

20. points of triangle: Bermuda, southern Florida, Puerto Rico

21. over 100 planes and ships vanished thus far

22. more than 1,000 lives lost thus far

23. no bodies or wreckage from any disappearances ever found

24. best known disappearance—five Navy Avenger bombers

25. pilots, expert flyers, on training mission, Florida, Dec. 5, 1945

26. pilots report gyro and magnetic compasses "going crazy"

27. flight leader to tower: "Can't see land, ocean looks strange, we're completely lost."

28. search produces no life rafts, no plane wrecks, no oil slicks

29. National Board of Inquiry said of bombers, "They vanished completely as if they had flown to Mars."

30. Navy supply ship U.S.S. Cyclops with crew of 309 vanished in good weather, March 4, 1918

31. no radio messages, no wreckage of ship found

32. time-space warp leading to other dimensions

33. electromagnetic force fields

34. UFOs from inner or outer space kidnap vessels

The Research Paper

1. Transactional Analysis Defined

2. Three People Inside of You: Parent, Adult, Child

3. Parent Ego State Defined

4. Adult Ego State Defined

5. Child Ego State Defined

6. Know Your Ego State: Your Feelings

7. Know Your Ego State: Your Words

8. Know Your Ego State: Your Actions

9. Know Your Ego State: Others' Reactions

10. Exchange of Strokes: Positive and Negative

11. Hunger for Strokes: Games

12. Applying What You Have Learned

13. 3	33. 3	57. 4
14. 4	34. 7	58. 5
15. 1	35. 6	59. 2
16. 2	36. 9	60. 1
	37. 1	61. 3
17. 5	38. 2	
18. 3	39. 4	62. 6
19. 2	40. 8	63. 5
20. 4	41. 5	64. 9
21. 1		65. 1
22. 6	42. 4	66. 2
	43. 5	67. 4
23. 3	44. 1	68. 3
24. 2	45. 3	69. 8
25. 5	46. 6	70. 7
26. 1	47. 2	
27. 4		71. 3
	48. 3	72. 4
28. 2	49. 1	73. 2
29. 3	50. 4	74. 5
30. 5	51. 2	75. 1
31. 4		
32. 1	52. 5	76. 3
	53. 4	77. 2
	54. 1	78. 4
	55. 2	79. 1
	56. 3	